The Physics of Emotions

By Cari Lynn Vaughn

Purple Rose Ink Publications

ISBN-13: 978-1530400447
ISBN-10: 1530400449

The Physics of Emotions

Introduction

INTRODUCTION

The Physics of Emotions was born out of dissatisfaction with the attitudes I found surrounding emotions and out of a need to understand my own emotions. None of the books that I consulted, and there were a great many, seemed to do the subject justice. I read out of a variety of genres searching for the answers to my questions, and no one genre contained the key. Instead, I found that by including a multitude of perspectives that I was finally able to grasp what I was looking for.

To give you a bit of background, I grew up going to a Christian church, but started reading New Age books as a teen. Shirley MacLaine was one of my favorite authors. Her book *Dancing In The Light* led me to Chris Griscom book *Ecstasy A New Frequency*. Griscom's book has been the most sophisticated and scientific "New Age" book that I've come ever across, and to this day my most frequent reference. *Dancing In The Light* also led me to read Gary Zukav's first book *The Dancing Wu Li Masters*. Zukav also made a connection between the science of quantum physics and the spiritual, which greatly influenced me.

The blending of Western rational and Eastern intuition has always held a certain fascination for me. Buddhism and the practice of yoga became entwined into my life as I entered college. Soon I discovered Jack Kornfield, Thich Nhat Hanh and the Dalia Lama. A few years later, while working at bookstore I found myself browsing the Science section. It was there that I found *The Physics of Consciences* by Evan Harris Walker and *The User Illusion* by Tor Norretranders. These wonderful books further bridged the gap between science and psychology for me.

I then blended all of these genres with my interests in Mythology, Wicca, and Feminism. Reading *Starhawk's Dreaming the Dark* and *Truth or Dare* allowed me see a new feminist approach to spirituality. When I came upon Anais Nin in the bookstore, I immediately identified with her. Her diaries and fiction have touched me deeply. In a time when men dominated psychology, she gave women a voice. Her work opened the doors for many generations of women to come.

As I continued to study, I found that the approaches to psychology and spirituality were definitely split. There was the tradition masculine view of the mind and then the feminine view of emotions. The masculine approach often stressed controlling thoughts and behaviors for a more rational and successful life. The feminine approach often allowed for more understanding and compassion and tended to stress letting nature take its course for a more satisfying personal life. I really wanted to reconcile these two approaches, but I wasn't sure how to do so.

The answer came through courses that I took in college. I was inspired by many of my English Literature courses and found that the metaphors in books and poetry were better able to explain my emotions and experiences than any nonfiction book I had encountered. I also took an Oceanography course for a required science credit, which surprisingly inspired me as well. It was then that I connected actual oceanography with the metaphor of the ocean. This connection was not entirely new, as Carl Jung had made references to it in many of his works, but never had anyone really explored this idea fully. In drawing some very specific analogies I found that I came into a much clearer idea of how emotions work. Suddenly, my life became a little less mysterious and little easier to understand. It was then I decided to share these insights

The first part of *The Physics of Emotions* examines first the definition of emotions and then the notion that emotion is energy, thereby subject to the laws of physics that govern energy. The second half explores the metaphor of the ocean and how we can use it to understand our own emotions. At the end, I explore the Seven Levels of Love.

You may find a comprehensive list of books in the back if you would like to follow my reading journey for yourself. I promise, you won't be disappointed!

"All Reality is Symbol for Sprit." ~Sufi Saying

Chapter 1: What Are Emotions?

Since humans have been aware they had emotions, they've been trying to figure out what they are. For a long time we humans acted on instinct, much like the animals around us, without a thought to the finer details. As we evolved, so did our understanding of what we felt.

Some of the first great thinkers identified emotions for us—putting words to what we didn't have words for before. Aristotle, Plato and many others began thinking, talking and writing about what they felt. But for them, the mind was supreme. It was our ability to be logical, rational and moral that set us apart from the animals we had dominion over. Emotions were acknowledged and explored, but it was the writer and poet's lot in life to explore the driving forces in our lives. Much of what was not understood was said to be fate or the hand of the gods.

It was Descartes who said, "I think therefore I am." He viewed emotion is impractical and unwanted, as did many philosophers who came after him. Thomas Aquinas, Emmanuel Kant, Rene Descartes, Edmund Husserl, Thomas Hobbes, David Hume, John Locke, Fredrich Nietzsche, Soren Kierkegaard and many others have examined life, society, religion and emotions place within those structures. However, none of them really took the time to define and work with emotions. It was Freud and his pupil Jung that began to delve into the world of feelings and analyze what they were and what they meant.

Nowadays, we lump emotions in with medicine and its branch of science known as Psychology. In fact, in order to get a definition of emotions, the most common place to go is a Medical dictionary. This is what the Medical Definition of Emotion is. 1: the affective aspect of consciousness. 2: a state of feeling. 3: a conscious mental reaction subjectively experienced as strong feeling usually directed toward a specific object and typically accompanied by physiological and behavioral changes in the body.

But what about Science? What does Science have to say about Emotions? Surprisingly, it has had little to say on the subject. Most of the Science surrounding emotions has been done in the area of Neurology. We are able to identify parts of the brain and their functions in relation to emotions. We know better than ever before how our brain works, but some of the nuances of our feelings are lost in these scientific explanations that have to do more with chemistry and electricity than consciousness.

Mystics have often felt like emotions are connected to our spiritual body and thus to the world of energy. They recognize that emotions cannot be controlled by thoughts alone. The emotional body is more powerful than we imagine. It isn't a small, unwanted part of ourselves, but a vast ocean inside. Chris Griscom says in her book *Ecstasy is a New Frequency* that, "What has not been understood until now is that the emotional body is an entity, an integral being with its own consciousness and its own laws of reality." (11)

The word emotion lends itself to defining itself in terms of energy. Emotions means *in-motion*. It comes from Latin for "*move out of*" and from the French for "*to stir up*." What are emotions if not energy in motion coming out of us or stirring within us? It is this last definition or way of looking at our feelings that I identify most with. If emotions are energy within us, then they are not as intangible and unworkable as we first thought. If we can understand how the microscopic world of quarks work, why not our emotions?

The medical definition just doesn't cover it. For the writer and the poet, emotions are a much more metaphysical thing that can only be explained through symbols and metaphors. Jung himself often used water as a symbol for the unconscious and our emotions, but he never really elaborated on it or followed the idea through. Why not use science not only to explain our emotions, but as a metaphor for them as well? But first, we need to discuss the language used to describe our emotions and how inadequate it is.

"My words are easy to know, and very easy to practice, but there is no one in the world who is able to know them and able to practice them." ~Lao Tse

Chapter 2: The Language of the Self

The dictionary isn't very helpful in this philosophical question of what emotions are, but it is a good place to begin. The Oxford English Desk Dictionary defines the self as: **Self**: *Combination form expressing reflexive action. It is of or directed toward ones self, by ones self, especially without external agency. On, in, for or relating to ones self.* As you can see, this does not accurately define what the self is. This reflexive pronoun was not meant to stand alone in a sentence. The philosophical idea of the self is not found in grammar or linguistics by itself, rather language allows for expression and exploration of the self. The self is not meant to self-contained. It is not something that can be grasped as a sole concept. Because of this, it is important to see what is combined with the word in order to begin getting the bigger picture. The self is always being defined by another word or words. In order to understand the word self we have to look beyond it. Know that the world *self* refers in this context to a person's identity, personality, consciousness, being, essence, soul, spirit, body or individuality.

There are endless combinations of the word self. Some are negative and some are positive. These combinations allow the world gain some sense of how we act or feel.

Positive Connotations	Negative Connotations
"less"	"ish"
Adjusting	Centered
Assertion	Abasement
Assured	Abuse
Confined	Destruct
Consciousness	Deception
Defense	Denial
Disciplined	Defeating
Employed	Delusion
Esteem (worth)	Esteem (vanity)
Evident	Doubt
Examination	Indulgence
Explanatory	Pity
Expression	Seeking*
Help	Interest
Educated	Inflicted
Sacrifice*	Sacrifice*
Knowledge	Induced
Worth	Justification
Taught	Proclaimed
Starter	Addressed
Made	Appointed
Control/Restraint*	Restraint*
Efficient	Critical
Aware	Efface

Two things trouble me about this list. First of all, there appears to be a conflict in society and in language with regard to the self. Selflessness and self-sacrifice are often advocated. Give up your identity and blend in to your relationship, family or society is the message conveyed subtly in our language. In recent years this message has been countered by our society, but the negative undercurrent is still there in our everyday vocabulary. We now recognize the dangers of losing one's identity or self to another. We call this codependent and consider it unhealthy. We promote, instead, a good self-esteem—self-esteem, being a good sense of worth, not vanity. Even still, there is a tendency to consider someone selfish or self-absorbed if they spend too much time working on themselves and trying to make themselves happy. The balance between the individual and the outside world has not yet been achieved.

There is a conflict between the inside and the outside, between the I and the you and between the individual and the collective. This conflict need not exist. Feeling selfish for focusing on yourself is something you need not feel. It is important to realize that there is no I *without* you. Individuals exist within the collective—separate yet connected. The perception that you have of yourself in relations to others is the key. No one is really isolated or alone, although at times it may feel like it. Others reflect your perceptions and feelings, as you reflect other's perceptions and feelings back at them. The world is your mirror. Use it. The better you understand others, the better you understand yourself. The better you understand yourself, the better you understand others.

The second problem with this list is while it shows how the self relates to world, there is no language to support the self separately. There just isn't a clear vocabulary for the emotional landscape that exists within. When you try to conjure up words to describe how you feel at any given time you find that words don't always convey the complexity of your emotions. I know they don't even begin to explain mine. When asked, most of us would come up with a rather elementary list of adjectives such as these:

Glad	Mad	Sad	Upset
Happy	Angry	Hurt	Worried
Excited	Indignant	Melancholy	Anxious
Pleased	Enraged	Mournful	Stressed
Hopeful	Hateful	Sorrowful	Eager
Pleased	Wrathful	Depressed	Uneasy
Cheerful	Ireful	Blue	Exhausted

I could go continue on with more synonyms, but that doesn't get us any further into the world of emotions. There are only minute distinctions between these words. Just as there is only a minute difference in definition between such words as compassion and sympathy, yet they are not always interchangeable.

For example, in Buddhism, **compassion** for all living things is taught as a way of life. The teachers and texts consistently use the word compassion and not sympathy. Why is that? Sympathy, in one of its definitions, is specifically used to mean the expression of sorrow for another's loss. This is part of, but completely what does having compassion for all living creatures mean. Compassion seems to have a more positive and general meaning. Compassion is also pity and mercy. Looking at the roots of these two words gives us a better understanding. *Sym* means alongside and *pat* means *to suffer*. We have emotions alongside someone else. Compassion comes from *com* meaning *with* and *pat* meaning *to suffer*. Compassion, more specifically, means deep awareness of the suffering of another and the wish to relieve it.

Empathy is different from compassion in that is not felt with or alongside someone else. Empathy means that your experience other's emotions as your own. You feel exactly what the other person feels. This is not the same as experiencing or relating to how someone else might feel or surrounding someone with your care and concern. Empathy is something that is not as common, but perhaps more important. It requires you to put yourself in their shoes and feel exactly what they are feeling.

Most of us don't take the time to deconstruct words to extract exact meanings. We use these words instinctively like a painter choosing what colors go on the canvas. So, I'd like to think of all these adjectives for words as the primary colors and all of their synonyms as the multitude of shades and tones of the rainbow. We choose which word seems to fit the best, but even that doesn't really express the energy that we feel inside. Emotion is something abstract that we try to make sense out of on a daily basis. We try to put a name to the ever-subtle moods that flow through us like water, but these names don't reflect the constant motion and evolution that we feel.

The definition of the word emotion is lacking as well. Simply put emotion is intense feeling. What then, I ask, are the less intense feelings called? Are they somehow not in the same category as emotions? The definition is lacking, but the key is to look at the word emotion itself. It is no mistake that it is spelled like it is. E-motion. It is energy in motion. If emotion is energy than why wouldn't it be subject to the same laws and principals that the energy of the universe? Understanding how energy works can help us understand how our emotions work. It is as simple and as complex as that.

"The human brain has 100 billion neurons, each neuron connected to 10 thousand other neurons. Sitting on your shoulders is the most complicated object in the known universe." ~ Michio Kaku

Chapter 3: Neurochemistry

Before we venture into the world of physics, we must take a detour into the world of Neurochemistry. Psychology has taken some quantum leaps in understanding how the brain works in recent years. Emotions have been explored through this blossoming field. My knowledge on this subject is somewhat limited, but a very interesting book called *Mind Wide Open* by Steve Johnson was a real mind opener for me. Johnson's book gave me yet another perspective to ponder.

In *The Mind Wide Open* Johnson explains that the neocortex is the emotional center of emotion in the brain. Humans and most animals have a neocortex and therefore are capable of feeling even the most basic emotions—specifically attachment. Reptiles do not have a neocortex and exhibit behavior drastically different from animals that do. For example, reptiles move from mate to mate without ever pairing up for any length of time. They do not have a life-mate and when they do have offspring they do not stay to raise them. They lay their eggs and move on. They have no attachments. Attachment and other emotions, have their origins in physiology.

The brain is responsible for sending and receiving chemical messages that are, at least in part, how our emotions are formed. Hormones do play a large part in our moods. Reproductive hormones, such as estrogen and testosterone, do affect our desires and cravings through a series of chemical reactions. There are a host of other hormones that work alongside these or independent of these.

Oxytocin is known as the *love* hormone. It is released primarily during labor, childbirth and during breastfeeding. It is said to help with bonding and attachment. It keeps new mothers feeling positive and peaceful in the face of some very tough times.

With the new diet aide Cortisol, more and more people have become aware of the stress hormone *corticosterone*. It is one of the hormones responsible for our flight or fight responses coming from the adrenal cortex. It does contribute to weight gain, but it also has many other affects as well. If someone is chronically stressed *corticosterone* can wear down the immune system and cause many health related problems.

Because it plays a large part in how antidepressant drugs work, the hormone *serotonin* has received attention as well. *Serotonin* is responsible for harm avoidance. *Dopamine* creates a sense of novelty seeking or pleasure seeking. Chronically low levels of *dopamine* can induce a drug addict's craving. *Norephinephrine* is responsible our reward dependence.

The three hormones *dopamine* and *norephinephrine, serotonin* creates a sort of biosocial personality. You could be a stay at home pleasure-seeker or a fearless reward dependent novelty seeker searching out for new experiences regardless of danger (154). The problem is that these hormones alone do not create a detailed or accurate picture of a person. They can help give us a glimpse in the function or dysfunction of a person, but there is something more elusive within our emotions.

Even when given medicine patients need counseling as well. Medication alone rarely solves a person's problems. Emotions can be traced to chemical reactions, but they are much more than that. Our thoughts and behaviors affect our brain chemistry just as our brain chemistry affects our thoughts and behaviors.

It is our consciousness that allows us some influence over an otherwise physical process. It is, in a way, mind over matter. So that leads us into the world of science, both in reality and metaphorically.

What exactly is chemistry? And what exactly is consciousness and how does it connect to the physical, mental, emotional and spiritual bodies that create what we call a self? How do thermodynamics, electrodynamics, quantum physics and string theory all factor in?

"Alchemy is a kind of philosophy: a kind of thinking that leads to a way of understanding." Marcel Duchamp

Chapter 3 Chemistry

Chemistry is a branch of science that studies the composition, structure, properties and change of matter. Matter consists of atoms and atoms consists of a core called the nucleus, which is surrounded by a space called the electron cloud. The nucleus is made up of positively charged protons and neutral neutrons, which have no charge.

Elements are rated by how many protons make up the nucleus. Hydrogen has one proton, Helium has two and so on. All elements in the Periodic Table are arranged and have a number from 1 to 118. Some of the heaviest are radioactive isotopes like uranium and plutonium.

Chemicals, which are broken down into atoms, can be bonded or broken apart with the addition of other chemicals. Take the common household elements of baking soda and vinegar for example. Baking soda and vinegar react with each other because of an acid-base reaction. Baking soda is a bicarbonate ($NaHCO_3$) and vinegar is an acetic acid (HCH_3COO). The combination of these products creates carbon dioxide.

In our emotional lives, we react to the various people and situations around us. Sometimes those reactions produce explosive or negative changes and other times they produce something new and wonderful. It all just depends on the individuals at play. When two people really click, they call it chemistry. More than anything, we have to take into consideration the fact that we never come out of these situation unchanged.

Chemistry came out the ancient art of Alchemy. In Medieval times the goal was to change led into gold or find an elixir that would grant immortality. We know these two goals are unrealistic now, but the idea of mixing and matching elements to create a change showed a great deal of creative and scientific potential.

The idea of transmutation in alchemy, which is a seemingly magical transformation, is very similar to the one that we go through in relationships. We attract people to us that will create the most changes in us. For example, if we admire the fact someone is outgoing, then hanging out them will help us become more outgoing. In turn, maybe the other person admires the fact that we are able to draw boundaries and take time for ourselves. Then we help them learn do the same.

"Our quest for the fabric of reality has brought us from religion to science. But that science, when asked to show us reality, has caused us to look into a mirror and see what we are." ~Evan Walker

Chapter 4: Consciousness

Evan Harris Walker connected Quantum Theories the search for the meaning of life in his 2000 book *The Physics of Consciousness.* He postulated that Newton's conception of reality was only the starting point in the search for truth.

The Quantum world is much more complicated than the old concepts of reality. It is a world where energy can be both particles and waves at the same time. Our very observation of its phenomenon changes its behavior. Things in the microscopic world do not work the way we think that they should work.

Our emotional Quirks are not that much unlike the particles labeled Quarks. Joy, Anger, Sadness and Disgust could easily fit into the idea of Quanta, Leptons, Mesons, Baryons and Mesons. Each of these particles plays a different role in our make-up, just like emotions.

The particles called Quanta help explain things like electro-magnetism and gravitation. These aggressive packets of light contain energy like that of our emotion anger. Leptons are small and light and emitted with electrons. They are perhaps the most similar to the emotion of joy. Baryons are heavy particles that are most similar to the emotion of sadness. Mesons hold things together and keep other things out like emotion of disgust.

Harris does not propose such an analogy, but it is not a far leap from his thoughtful mediation on how the world of particles is broken down. What Harris does do, is to move into the idea of Consciousness.

Consciousness is not thinking. It is not thinking about being Conscious even. It is not the act of being self-reflective. So if Consciousness is not related to thinking then what is it? It is our experiences as filtered through all of our senses. It isn't thinking about those experiences, but the raw data contained within those moments. It is what makes up our knowledge of the world around us and inside of us. It is things in their entirety and it is reality. But more than that, it is the FEEL of things. And when one is conscious not just of their thoughts, but of consciousness itself, that is enlightenment.

The embodiment of Consciousness can be found, it seems, where Zen Buddhism and Science intersect. Buddhism has often come to the same answers as Science earlier and intuitively, but the answers are often the same nonetheless.

The Tao of Physics by Fritjof Capra explains this concept most beautifully. Capra says that they central aim of Eastern Mysticism is to experience all the phenomenon in the world as manifestations of the same ultimate reality. Every individual consciousness can tap into what Jung calls The Collective Unconscious and understand the essence of all things. The Hindus call it Brahman and the Buddhists call it Dharmakaya or Tathata and the Taoists simply call it Tao.

"My investment of time, as an educator, in my judgment, is best served teaching people how to think about the world around them. Teach them how to pose a question. How to judge whether one thing is true versus another. What the laws of physics say." ~Neil deGrasse Tyson

Chapter 5: Physics

In 1687 scholar Sir Isaac Newton revolutionized science when he formulated the three basic laws of physics. These *Laws of Physics* are concerned with the interactions between basic forces and materials. For the most part Newton dealt with gravity and its effects on the light, the earth, and anything of that consists of matter. These are Newton's laws and the corresponding emotional law.

1st Law. The first law is the *Law of Inertia*. Things in motion tend to stay in motion until some outside force brings it to a stop.

Emotions will always continue to move within you unless you are aware of them and able to express and then change them. The outside force in this case would be consciousness. Once conscious of your feelings you can then express them. Ex-press. Meaning to press outward. The emotions are inside and need to be pushed outside in some form or another. Talking and writing are two very good ways to do this, but there are other ways of expressing yourself. Painting, drawing, dancing, singing, and any activity that is creative can serve as a positive outlet. Focusing on a project or exercising vigorously can help as well.

One of the most common problems is that a person will try to ignore, suppress or control unwanted feelings. This does not stop the inertia of the emotion. The emotion will keep moving inside, turning, and bouncing, which will cause chaos. Emotion must be expressed in order to make it stop moving.

2nd Law. The second law is the *Law of Force Equals Mass Times Acceleration.* A change in speed results in imbalance and acceleration. Mass will move toward the imbalance.

If there is an emotional imbalance, emotions will accelerate and intensify. The more intense an emotion it is, the more intense the situation and the more dramatic it will become. The larger the emotion, the more issues there will be surrounding it. The more issues you have to deal with, the more mass there is. The more mass you have, the heavier the emotion. You will be focused on these heavy emotions because the imbalance will direct attention to itself. Everything gets pulled down under the gravity of these emotions.

This is particularly evident when you see find yourself repeating the same set of situations over and over. You'll keep attracting the same type of people to you and the same set of circumstances until the issues and emotions are dealt with completely. It is important to recognize patterns that you might be stuck in. What is pulling you down and why? What fears can you push out to lighten your emotional life?

3rd Law. The third law is the *Law For Every Action there is an Equal and Opposite Reaction.*

Newton's third law is Karma and the balance of the universe. Karma is often misunderstood as punishment for wrongdoing, but it is more than that. Karma works like a credit and debit system. It is a record of all your deeds, good and bad.

31

If you think and act negatively then more negative things will come your way. You will keep adding to your emotional and spiritual debt until you are consumed with no easy way out. There is no karmic loophole like bankruptcy.

The more aware you become of your actions, the quicker they come back at you. Sometimes it may take years, even lifetimes, to see how your actions affect you, but sometimes it can work instantly.

Gravity adheres to Newton's Third Law as well. Gravity is what keeps us tethered to Earth and, in turn, to each other. However, that energy sometimes creates friction is we struggle against it.

Ancients observed the night sky above us and watched as the plants came and went. Eventually Galileo Galilei worked out that it was Gravity that pulled the planets around the sun in their elliptical orbits. And it was gravity that kept us from flying right off the earth as it spun around and around.

The band Enigma has a song called "The Gravity of Love." The lyrics talk about how experience is key to surviving the gravity of love. It speaks of love as a force that compels us toward one another. And although it may be a tumultuous experience, peace is possible once we give in and stop fighting.

Einstein proposed his theory of relativity in 1907. He observed that gravity appeared to warp around planets and black holes. He recognized that gravity not only effected space, but time as well. In his special theory of relativity ($E=MC2$), he explored the idea that mass can become equivalent to energy. Even a little bit of mass, like an atom, contains a large amount of energy. That idea is what led to the Atomic Bomb. However, some energy will be lost in the conversion.

Emotionally, we see that our bodies are made of matter, but inside them is an extraordinary amount of energy. The only way to release all that energy is become aware of the vast internal world that exists in all of us. We have untapped emotional energy that can offer us great power. But with great power comes great responsibility. If we blind ourselves and cut off our connection to our emotional world, it can create something akin to an atomic bomb inside of us. But if we know how to work with the energy, we won't find ourselves exploding or self-destructing.

Mechanics is the study of the motions of bodies. Can also be applied to human physical bodies or emotional bodies. In classic Physics Mechanics they study various variables such as position, angle, velocity, acceleration, jerk, momentum, torque, power and energy. Although Classic Physics observes larger bodies in motion, it also extends to the microscopic world.

The Mechanics of Emotions deals with what is observable. We can't see love, but we can see its effects. Certain actions will indicate how we feel. From a text to a hug, that energy must manifest somehow. Desire itself is not tangible, but we feel it in a loved one's kiss and in their touch.

Light is an electromagnetic radiation. It travels in waves and yet within the waves are tiny packets of particles or quanta. It is unique duality. Although light has much in common with thermodynamics, it is primarily studied by those in Quantum Physics.

Light is also associated with God, Love and the Soul. Light represents the divinity within us and our spiritual side. We all have an electromagnetic frequency that we vibrate at. We are all part of the divine energy that is God, the Universe or whatever you want to call it. And we can tap into that divine energy.

According to Chris Griscom, we don't just have a physical, mental and emotional body, but a spiritual one as well. Light is what represents our spiritual body. And often we can only affect change in our lives when we change our spiritual body. We recognize our issues in our physical or mental body first. We might see it goes deeper to an emotional or spiritual issue, but until we have some sort of spiritual change—our emotional body often remains stuck. This is why trying to change our emotions with our thoughts isn't always enough.

"Just as the constant increase of entropy is the basic law of the universe, so it is the basic law of life to be ever more highly structured and to struggle against entropy."

~Vaclav Have

Chapter 6: Thermodynamics

Thermodynamics is the branch of Physics concerned with heat and temperature—specifically the transfer of energy. Both heat and temperature are often used to describe that nature of love, passion and relationships. When thinking in terms of energy one has to keep in mind the factors of entropy and pressure. However, in both Science and relationships, equilibrium is the idealized state for heat and temperature.

Heat one of the things studied and measured in physics. More equals more energy and cold equals less energy.

Heat is the passionate fire of creativity. It is our connection to the earth and to the physical expression of our emotions. When we feel energetic we call it being *fired up*. When we talk about passion we talk about *the heat of the moment*.

There are four kinds of systems in Thermodynamics. First is the States of a System. This has to do with variables related to the type of system involved. For example, a bath would be a system and the state of it would be the temperature and all the changes taking place in the bathtub from the time the tap is turned on until it has cooled and, ultimately drained. We often talk about the state of our relationships—are then doing good or bad or are they merely okay.

The walls of the system are something else to consider. In our example of the bathtub, the walls would be the plastic walls that contain the water. It should be solid and durable enough to contain the water and heat of that water for a considerable amount of time. It would not be good if the plastic was cracked or made of inferior material that was damaged by the heat of the water. So it goes with relationships as well. Only, our walls might be damaged by our emotions. Past experiences might have cracked or warped out walls.

Then there are the set of thermodynamics of a particular system. This would be the dynamic of a particular relationship. How is the give and take? What particular rules apply and what rules must be thrown out? It is different for each closed system of thermo-dynamics and it is different for each relationship involved.

If thermodynamics represent the exchange of energy of our emotions and energy we exchange in relationships, then we can take that metaphor a step further.

The First Law of Thermodynamics is simply the law of conservation of energy and mass. Applied for thermodynamic systems, the law of conservation of energy states that the total energy of an isolated system is constant. Energy can be transformed from one form to another, but cannot be created or destroyed.

This means anything you might feel cannot be created or destroyed. Relationships may come and they may go, but the energy poured into that relationship cannot be destroyed. The energy lies inside of you and is merely expressed through relationships.

Desire, love and need can be transformed into anger, hatred and disgust. By the same token, anger, hatred and disgust can be transformed back into desire, love and need. Whatever is felt toward someone will swing from one extreme to other until equilibrium is found.

The only way to be free of the heat of a particular relationship is to follow the emotions through as the molecules of emotions slow down and the furious bouncing back and forth ceases. Heat will seek to spread throughout the system until it is evenly distributed, thus the heat of desire will seek to find a balance inside us. Only when enough time has passed and things have cooled, will the intensity lessen and a peace will be found with that person or relationship.

But do not be mistaken—if you love someone the essence of those feelings will always remain in some form or another. The best case scenario here is to come to peace with those feelings. Burying them or ignoring them will not work. Balance is the goal—not annihilation of the entire system.

The second law is a straightforward law of physics with the consequence that, in a closed system, you can't finish any real physical process with as much useful energy as you had to start with — some is always wasted. This means that a perpetual motion is impossible. The second law was formulated after nineteenth century engineers noticed that heat cannot pass from a colder body to a warmer body by itself.

The Second Law of Thermodynamics also deals with **Entropy** Second Law of Thermodynamics: In any cyclic process the entropy will either increase or remain the same.

A perfect system would have a temperature of absolute zero. At the absolute zero of temperature, there is zero thermal energy or heat. Since heat is a measure of average molecular motion, zero thermal energy means that the average atom does not move at all. When none of the atoms which make up a perfectly ordered system don't move at all, there can be no disorder or different states possible for the system.

An emotional body can never be perfectly still. Apathy is the total lack of feelings and total lack of motion in an emotional body. It has been my experience that some people can flip a switch and allow themselves to turn off their emotions temporarily. It is a defense mechanism against being totally overwhelmed with emotions. However, this is not something that can be maintained over a long period of time. Total apathy or absolutely zero emotions is a state that is inhuman. Once those emotions switch off for good, we are as good as dead ourselves.

Sometimes grief, pain, anger and hatred can be so intense that we go into an emotional shock. We become numb and feel cut off from all feelings. This is a most dangerous place to be because it can result in either suicide or murder. A depressed person will become suicidal, but a sociopath will become homicidal.

Either way, the numbness is similar to how people go into shock after a physical injury. Pain allows us to know we are alive and that something is broken or wrong. Once that pain is gone along with all the other feelings, a person will feel dead inside. Recovery from this is possible, but it takes time. A person has to become unstuck and learn to feel again.

Entropy is a measure of the amount of energy which is unavailable to do work. Entropy is also a measure of the disorder of a system. Entropy can measure of the multiplicity of a system.

Entropy is wasted energy and opportunity. There is a potential amount of energy to be spent. If the energy is not spent then the energy is diffused and dissipated. It becomes difficult, if not impossible, to find a way to tap into that unused potential energy. Scientists measure the amount of unused energy and call it entropy.

This idea is particularly important as far as emotions go. Entropy is emotional chaos. It is loss of purpose. This happens when you don't express your emotions. Say, for example, that you never told father or mother how angry and hurt you really felt growing up. Then you never told your girlfriend or boyfriend how hurt and angry they made you. Instead, you bottle it up. Thinking you put it in the past, you moved on. The problem is that the emotions were never released. You never screamed, cried or talked through your emotions. All of the energy that was created was never spent. Years down the road you wonder why you feel so hurt and angry still. Your emotions seem random and chaotic. There doesn't seem to a purpose or pattern to them. This is entropy.

Chaos Theory deals with slight variations of pattern. If a mathematical formula, which has a predicable correct answer, is varied slightly then the answer will not be what is expected. Instead of a neat predictable pattern, the pattern becomes a double spiral of variations.

This phenomenon has been observed in many different fields, including, meteorology, ecology, and economics. It also has been observed, although not specifically identified, in psychology. Chaos occurs in our lives in much the same way as it does elsewhere. We get off course somewhere along the way and our pattern changes. It then keeps repeating in a double spiral until we are able to change it. We keep getting into unhealthy relationships and finding ourselves facing the same problems in slightly different situations. Getting out of these patterns isn't easy at all.

The only way out of chaos is through awareness. You have to be conscious of your particular pattern and work to change it. Understanding what you are doing and why is the only way to put a stop to the pattern. Then you have to express whatever emotions you've repressed. They may be weeks, months, years, or even decades old, but it doesn't matter. As long as you hold them inside, they will remain with you.

It may come natural to hold them inside. Perhaps you are afraid of hurting others with your emotions or perhaps you are afraid that expressing these negative thoughts and feelings will make you a bad person. There are many reasons for keeping things to yourself. It doesn't matter why in the end. It just matters that an unexpressed emotion will cause chaos. If you don't say what you feel when you feel it, then entropy occurs.

The most difficult thing then becomes figuring out how to say what you feel without stepping into the blame game. Too often we blame others for our problems and don't take responsibility for our actions. In order to be healthy and productive, you must learn to be tactful and diplomatic in your expression. Explain to those around you that these are your feelings and ask that they be respected. Don't try to manipulate, control or change others through your expression. The only thing that you can do is put your feeling out there and let them go. Just letting people know that you are hurt, angry or frustrated really can change a lot of things by itself.

"The kingdom of heaven is like electricity. You don't see it. It is within you." ~Maharishi Mahesh Yogi

Chapter 7: Electrodynamics

Electrodynamics is a branch of theoretical physics that studies the interactions between electric charges and currents using an extension of the classical Newtonian Model. Electricity is the set of physical phenomena associated with the presence and flow of electric charge. In other words, Electricity then has to do with the transfer of energy and the transmission of electrons. Electricity has a wide variety of effects, such as lightning, static electricity, electromagnetic induction and electric current.

Electrically charged matter or particles are produces, electro-magnetic fields. These particles can be positive, negative or neutral. Electrons have a negative charges, while Protons have a positive charge. Neutrons are neutral. These three elements are the building blocks for what we know as the atom and it is crucial to electricity.

Our attraction to others can have a positive, negative or neutral effect on us. Sometimes we try to be with someone who repels us and disaster follows. But being with someone who causes no effect whatsoever can be just as damaging. It is the positive charge or the positive change we see in ourselves that creates the most power.

Electrons can be made to move from one atom to another. When those electrons move between the atoms, a current of electricity is created. The electrons move from one atom to another by way of flowing back and forth.

Electricity courses invisibly through the ground, air or wires and isn't seen until that connection is broken. Then the electricity jumps and we see that spark.

Love is energy and that energy is very much like electricity in as much that electricity is often naked to the human eye, but its effects are unmistakable. We operate as a closed system until someone comes along and makes us feel like we are incomplete without them. Our spark jumps, leaps and bridges the gap between two people. The connection is made and then two people create a new closed system—a new dynamic.

"I am large. I contain multitudes." ~Walt Whitman, Song of Myself

Chapter 9 Quantum Physics

Quantum Physics studies the behavior of particles, which are the microscopic building blocks of all life. Max Planck is credited with the discovery of Quantum Mechanics, so Planck's Constant is a good place to begin.

The formula known as Planck constant links the amount of energy a photon carries with the frequency of its electromagnetic wave. It is an important quantity in quantum physics. This formula has been used in many, many calculations since its inception.

The television show *Lost* used this concept. Faraday, named after Physicist Michael Faraday, finds one person to hold onto while time traveling. Having one person as his constant anchored him and kept him from going completely mad. Later, Desmond finds his constant in Penny Widmore.

While it is unlikely we will experience time travel in our life time, we do need a constant to anchor us. That constant may be our father, mother, sister, brother or another family member. It may be our best friend or our spouse. It is this person who shows us loyalty and unconditional love. When we were struggling and consumed by our emotions, their light and love that reminds us of our place and our purpose.

Sometimes a constant may not even be a living person or a person in our lives currently. The memory or idea given to us may be enough to carry us through the darkest times. It is the principle that we use to measure ourselves and the world around us that is our constant. Whatever we find embodies this principle will be our constant—our guide on our emotional and spiritual journeys.

In any case, Planck realized that even black bodies such as blackholes radiate a minimal amount of energy. Planck also noticed that when a light shone onto a metal surface, electrons emit light back. This reflective effect is why the moon appears to glow.

This shows us that even the darkest of times and the darkest of people still have something to offer us. We can still receive their energy and use them as reflections to learn from. I first read about the idea of using the world as a mirror for our inner world in Shakti Gawain's book *Living in The Light*.

When you are in conflict with a family member, co-worker or friend, stop and ask yourself what is it that this conflict is trying to teach you? Whatever issue you have with them is something you need to work on within yourself. Instead of seeing them as the problem, you see them as an aspect of yourself that you don't like or can't accept. Once you come to peace with that aspect of yourself, then the issue may dissipate and you can move on.

Now, Particles are unstable and tend to change and fluctuate as they are observed. It is theorized that the mere observation of the particles changes their behavior. The Heisenberg Uncertainty Principle states that it is impossible to know simultaneously the exact position and momentum of a particle. That is, the more exactly the position is determined, the less known the momentum, and vice versa.

The Uncertainty Principle means that it is impossible to know exactly where you are at in a relationship without knowing where the relationship is going. The paradox is that trying to define your position in any given relationship will ultimately make the path of that relationship less clear. Trying to predict if a relationship will last or rather it will end directly effects that relationship and makes its natural course increasingly difficult to discern.

Relationships require faith. Instead of trying to predict and control the outcome of your emotional experiment, letting go is the only way to know the natural results. If you love the other person, you will always love them. However, there are many other factors that can push people together or tear them apart. Past experiences may give us some idea of what to expect, but those past experiences will not always predict other relationships and other dynamics. By assuming our partner will hurt us or leave us, we often make it so. Our thoughts and observations often shape our actions for the worst. But they don't have to. We can let go of expectations and live in the moment. It is only when we live in that moment that love will fulfill its capacity to surprise us and lead us to new places inside and outside of ourselves.

Another paradox often talked about it Quantum Physics is Schrödinger's Cat. Schrödinger proposed a thought experiment in order to point out the flaws in Quantum Theories. A cat imagined as being enclosed in a box with a radioactive source and a poison that will be released when the source unpredictably emits radiation. The cat is considered to be simultaneously both dead and alive until the box is opened and the cat observed.

We can't know the outcome of our experiments in life, love and Quantum Physics until the end. There is no way to predict the path we will take, so why try? There is so much out of our conscious control and potentially unlimited possibilities that thinking about it can weigh us down.

We all like to play the "what if?" game. Philosophers and Psychologists calls these what ifs Counterfactuals. Our thoughts take us to places that counter or contradict the facts. Some Quantum Physicists like to think that all of these possibilities are actual realities in other worlds or parallel universes.

The book *If Only: How To Turn Regret Into Opportunity* by Neil Roese explores this phenomenon. Our ability to speculate is dependent on a healthy use of imagination. However, you can beat yourself up over what you did or didn't do. Blaming yourself is not healthy, but the use of Counterfactuals can be helpful if you do it correctly. Counterfactuals are a way to create meaning in our lives. Only by comparing and contrasting what did happen with what could have happen, can we truly understand our choices. Don't dwell or overthink these comparisons because that can all too easily lead you down the road to depression. Roese tells us that we can use the exercise to better our future choices and move on though. Always keep your eye on the bigger picture he reminds us.

Chris Griscom would call this "Holographic Thinking." When we can see more than just the facts, we can make more sophisticated choices. Seeing the big picture with all the possibilities allows to grow in ways we never dreamed possible

"If there was nothing wrong in the world, there would be nothing for us to do." ~George Bernard Shaw

Chapter 10 Antimatter

For a long time antimatter was just a theory. But then the Physicists were able to detect them in space. Eventually the Physicist at CERN were able to create antimatter in their giant Hadron Collider.

It appears as if the world and nearly everything in it is made up of matter, but it is thought that maybe the large vast emptiness of space is filled with antimatter.

In any case, when matter and antimatter happen to collide, they not only cancel each other out, but they annihilate one another. So if an electron and a positron meet with a bang, then neither one will survive.

This process can release a great deal of energy all at once. Scientists hope that space travel could be fueled by antimatter engines, while others hope to use it as a weapon. We've not been able to produce enough or experiment with it enough to make it work for us yet.

Matter and Antimatter have important symbolic significance in our lives. We are already aware of the great many opposites that are at play in our lives. We have light and dark, day and night and yin and yang—among many others. Matter and Antimatter are opposites at the most minuscule microscopic level.

Emotions work in the same way. Some people say the opposite of love is hate, but I would disagree. Hatred is merely the opposite of

Desire. Some say the opposite of love is apathy. But apathy is more the absence of feelings in general—not any one feeling in particular. No, if love is our emotional matter, then it is fear that is our emotional antimatter.

Fear and Love churn inside of us, but rarely do they collide. We find that far too often we are being driven by the negative feeling in our lives. Decisions are made because we fear the alternatives. We avoid relationships because we fear being hurt. We avoid being vulnerable because we fear being annihilated.

Fear isolates us and controls us, but it is not our natural state of being. It is love, light and matter that make us who are. Our greatest power comes in releasing our fears—annihilating our hang ups and issues in this life.

Fear can't be avoided. It will always be there, waiting for you. You can put off dealing with something and you can pretend it doesn't exist, but eventually it will catch up to you. Facing your fears is your best bet.

Collide those antimatter particles with matter particles. Be brave and surround yourself with compassion, love and understanding. Don't judge and hate yourself. Don't let the negativity of others and yourself overwhelm you. Fight to annihilate any hint of self-doubt.

Knowledge is power. In this case, the ability to combat fear with love. We must peer into the darkness, acknowledge its existence, then, and only then, we can bombard those negative emotions with positive ones. The light of truth releases us and gives us more power than we ever imagined possible.

"When we understand string theory, we will know how the universe began. It won't have much effect on how we live, but it is important to understand where we come from and what we can expect to find as we explore." ~Stephen Hawking

Chapter 11 String Theory

During the 1960s and 1970s a new theory was developed as an extension of Quantum Physics. Hundreds of Physicist began working on these theories and created the Super String Theory of the 1980s and 1990s.

String Theory makes an effort to combine the Classic Physics of Gravity with the new Theories of Quantum Physics. Sometimes it is referred to as the Theory of Everything or TOE.

String theory describes how strings circulate through space and interact with each other. In one version of the theory, there is only one kind of string, which may look like a small loop or segment of ordinary string, and it can vibrate in different ways.

One of the major implications of String Theory is that allows for multiple dimensions, multiverses and many worlds. It is also the theory that provides for the existence of wormholes.

This is good news for our inner worlds. Counterfactuals may be a reality in another universe. Relationships that didn't work out in this life, may have worked out in another reality. We may have made a different set of decisions that led to a different life entirely.

Reincarnation has been a key belief in Hinduism, Buddhism and other religions since ancient times. But what if they aren't past lives so much as parallel lives?

This means that our soul is like a string and it vibrates through many universes and many lives. Because we all are made up of a sort of divine spark, we are connected to the universe and everything else within in it. We may feel isolated and all alone in the world, but on a sub-atomic level, we are part of the infinite.

Knowing that we a part of the universe and everything in it is not only comforting, but important for improving our world. That knowledge that everyone is you and you are everyone makes it easier to practice kindness and compassion. So much ugliness, hatred and violence comes out of feeling detached. When we can view someone as an "other" it is much easier to hurt them. But when you take to heart that whatever you do to them is like doing it to yourself, then you are a lot less likely to do harm to anyone.

Classical Physics describes how gravity works and Quantum Physics describes how particles work, but there was a discrepancy between the two fields of study. The rules that appear to apply on the microscopic level don't appear to apply to macroscopic level. String Theory begins to merge these two very different sets of rules.

String Theory also theorizes about the existence of the Graviton. The Graviton is a proposed particle that is weightless and has an unlimited range. It would the power behind gravity. But like light, it would be made up packets of particles that travel in waves in what is known as a Gravitation wave.

Scientists have observed Gravitational Waves here on earth through large bodies of water like the ocean, but until recently they haven't been able to prove that gravity travels in waves across the empty space of the universe as well.

These long, low frequency waves can penetrate areas that electromagnetic waves cannot. It is thought that these waves could merge blackholes and other objects. Perhaps it is these gravitons and gravitational waves that get us through our own dark times. These so-called weak forces can be our thread through time.

Thomas Moore explores these dark times in his book *Dark Night of the Soul*. It was originally St. John of the Cross that introduced to the idea of our own personal spiritual hell that we had to find our way through. St John and Thomas Moore let us know that we are not alone and provide some guidance through their writing.

Some people spend their lives running from their problems or trying to outsmart them. But the only way out is through. It may take us a long time, but a force like gravity can pull us through the darkest holes if we only have faith. If we know that the wave will carry us through if we let it, then we can pass through even the darkest of black holes. We may lose our job, our house, our car, our friends and our family. We may even lose our identity, but there is always a force that will keep us going. Call it momentum, call it determination or call it will power. Whatever it is, the human spirit's capability for survival is unparalleled.

"The sea is the favorite symbol for the unconscious, the mother of all that lives." ~Carl Jung, From Archetypes of the Unconscious

Chapter 12: Oceanography

Oceanography is the study of the ocean. It overlaps with a lot of other branches of science, including: astronomy, biology, chemistry, climatology, geography, geology, hydrology, meteorology and physics

The Ocean is a living body of energy like our emotions and thus the perfect metaphor. Emotions ebb and flow like the tides. Everything Flows and Moves in Cycles like the tides and currents.

Tides are created by gravity essentially, but the Sun, Moon and Earth are all factors in its rise and fall. Then when the Moon is closer to the Earth, the tides rise—but only by a couple of inches. The sun's gravitational pull is stronger, but the sun is further away from the Earth. When the Sun and Moon are both closer to the Earth than normal, the tides will be exceptionally high. The rotation of the Earth, or the Coriolis Effect, and the location of the shore in relation to the equator will also factor in.

This means Love, Fear and our Physical Body all have an effect on our emotions. We have many things pulling at us, but it is not random. The Light of Love is the strongest pull on us, but it is often further out of reach. Fear is often closer to our heart, but its pull isn't as strong as Love's pull. When Love and Fear are both close to our hearts, then we will be extremely emotional. In addition, our neurochemistry will also factor in to our emotional state.

The Ocean is powerful and can break down even the strongest rocks on the shore, given enough time. It is slow but sure, and cannot be ignored. The shore is constantly changing because erosion changes the shape of the shore. The tides deposit shells and debris, but takes sand and other things back with it. It is a constant give and take that can be used to our advantaged, but never tamed or harnessed

Newton's First Law also apply to water as well as other bodies. Things is motion tend to stay in motion, unless stopped by an outside force. This is true of waves as much as it is our emotions. Emotions tend to move through us continuously until changed by thoughts and by our spirit ultimately.

Underneath the water are Currents and Currents bring nutrients from earth to the top. The Movement of Emotions brings Creative Force to life. Ice in the sea, that part of us that is always frozen. A little bit melts and raises our depth. We shine the light of love on our frozen emotions and become deeper than before, but there is always the threat of flooding

There are also columns of water that exist within the great body of the ocean. Heavy water sinks to the bottom and the lighter floats to the top. The top water grows cold and sinks to the bottom, letting the water that was on the bottom rise to the top. Heat and cold keep water moving in cycles. Fear and love keep emotions moving.

The water that is denser can create a stream, like the Gulf Stream. This inner stream of water represents the more dense emotions. The stronger and deeper the emotion, the more likely it will be that it will continue to carry you along no matter what the outside weather is like. Issues from childhood, a particular relationship can be like that Gulf Stream.

There are vortexes and eddies that can form in the sea of our emotions. Eddies are created when a pocket of dense water begins to rotate within itself, and lighter water cannot penetrate it. The regular water moves around it, but the eddy just continues to move within itself.

Emotions will do this as well. A particular feeling will get stuck and even though you continue on with life, this feeling never goes anywhere. It remains inside you, turning and turning. The eddy will dissipate on its own without you even being aware of it, or you might become caught in it. When you find yourself caught in this cycle of emotions it can be quite frustrating. You begin to get dizzy and confused and unsure of how to get out of the swirling water. It often takes a great deal of strength to pull yourself from the vortex and into the water outside, but it can be done.

The Temperature of the sea changes much slower than that of the air and land. Emotions change much slower than thoughts (which is represented by the air/wind).

"Water is the driving force of all nature."

~ Leonardo da Vinci

Chapter 13 Composition of Salt Water

The ocean is composed of many things. The water itself is made up of H20. This means it is two parts hydrogen and one part oxygen. Hydrogen is perhaps the simplest and most common element in the universe, but it needs oxygen to become water. Oxygen is the third most common element in the universe.

In terms of emotions we can think of Hydrogen as our ego or sense of self. The other Hydrogen can be like our Super Ego. Oxygen is our Id. Freud used the idea of Ego, Superego and Id to explain our relationship to ourselves in society. The Super Ego is our moral center—our idealized self. The Id, on the other hand, is our wild untamed self.

But water is rarely pure. Most water contains particles and other elements. In the ocean the three most common elements are Sodium, Chloride and Magnesium. Sodium and Chloride are salt essentially.

Sodium, like tears, is a necessary part of life. But too much of it can be a bad thing. Chloride is a more aggressive element and could be considered the element of anger in our emotional make-up. Magnesium is perhaps the most versatile and powerful element, which would make it similar to joy.

Sulfates and Calcium are also found in Sea Water to a lesser degree. Sulfates are various other types of salts and are acidic in nature. These salts are the various types of sorrows we experience in life. These sorrows and frustrations are not the same. Jealousy, envy, bitterness and grief are not all one sorrow, but many.

Calcium is the fifth-most-abundant dissolved ion in seawater. It also happens to be the element that is needed by creatures living in the ocean. Humans need calcium as well. It builds strong bones, among other things.

Calcium then is equal to what helps us grow the most in our emotional lives. It is the build-up of friendships and other attachments. It is affection and need.

Amino Acids are also found in Sea Water. They are the building blocks of life. These complex little structures are beginnings of our own inner life. They can represent the complexity of how we feel toward a person or event in our lives. Amino Acids represent how we can feel attraction, attachment, affection and trust all at the same time. Or how we can feel attachment along with distrust and bitterness. Or how we can feel trust along with anger.

Because of these all these elements, salt water is an excellent conductor of electricity—aka love or divine energy. Love is not just an emotion to be lumped with others, rather it is merely the conduit through which we feel and express that love.

"Those who enter the gates of heaven are not beings that have no passions or who have curbed their passions, but those who have cultivated an understanding of them."

~William Blake

Chapter 14 Marine Biology

A large proportion of all life on Earth lives in the ocean, which covers 71% of the surface. Marine Biology is the study of all the life within Earth's many waters. Habitats include coral reefs, kelp forests, seagrass meadows, the surrounds of seamounts and thermal vents, tidepools, muddy, sandy and rocky bottoms, and the open ocean. Organisms studied range from microscopic phytoplankton and zooplankton to huge whales.

There is a large ecosystem under the water just as there is a large ecosystem operating inside of us. It is vast and varied. The Sea Plants and Creatures are equal to the personality that we project. It is the ego. It is a part of our inner landscape, adding character. It is the people, situations and life that we create for ourselves. The life we allow inside are essentially the people who inhabit our outside lives. Your mom, dad, brother, sister, grandmother, grandfather, uncle, aunt, cousins, husband, wife, kids etc. all have their emotional counterpart inside.

It has been only recently that we've been able to traverse the deepest parts of the ocean. The deepest recorded oceanic trench measured to date is the Mariana Trench, near the Philippines, in the Pacific Ocean at 35,840 ft. At such depths, the water pressure is intense and there is no sunlight, but some life still manages exists. Among the creatures found down there are: white flatfish, a shrimp and a jellyfish were seen by the American crew of the bathyscaphe Trieste when it dove to the bottom in 1960

This shows us that even in the dark recesses of our emotional being, things are constantly moving and changing. The volcanic vents on the bottom of the sea. Strange creatures who live off of the heat, rather than light thrive. Inside our emotions there are strange creatures dwelling in that dark place as well. These are our peccadilloes, fetishes and other dark desires.

If the sea didn't exist life wouldn't exist, not as we know it. We need the water that evaporates from the ocean to become the rain. We need the food and natural resources that comes from the sea. Essentially we would be living on a desert planet if the sea did not exist.

But it does exist, physically and symbolically. Our emotions do exist, and rather we chose to dwell in them or not, we need them. We need emotions to connect us to the water, to the source of life. We are no more than carbon without water and without our emotions.

Having said that, there is something to be said for being consumed by the ocean, by emotions. We are creatures who also need air and need rational thought. Too many emotions can drown a person, but too much air can dry up a person. A balance must be struck in order to survive. Just the right mixture of thoughts and feelings must be found so that harmony can prevail.

"Beings are in a dynamic state of change and life is process. In daily life we find no constant. Movement is a continuum from one extreme to its opposite. Process occurs as movement between these poles of the universe. The poles are complementary; one can't live without the other. The universe is constituted of an endless to-and-fro movement of life from any pole to its complementary opposite." ~Nahum Stiskin, *The Looking Glass God*

Chapter 15 Islands in the Sea

Islands are generally small masses of dry land in the middle of water. Islands are not continents though. Continents are understood to be large, continuous, discrete masses of land, ideally separated by expanses of water.

Oceanic islands are ones that do not sit on continental shelves. The vast majority are volcanic in origin. The Hawaiian Islands are good examples of this. There are several types of Oceanic Islands, including ones that are part of an arc, ones that appear when a rift surfaces and ones that are positioned over tectonic plate hotspots.

If the Earth itself represents are physical bodies, then islands are small manifestations of our emotional bodies. Sometimes we need to stretch our sea legs and walk on dry land. Sometimes we need a break from our emotional worlds.

These island getaways can take the form of any number of things. It can be any sort of physical activity from sports to exercise to sex. We need physical releases to save us from drowning in our seas of feeling or oceans of emotion.

Like the Volcanoes that often form Ocean Islands, our need for release can be about a fiery need for passion and creativity. Creating art, music or a piece of writing may not be as physically demanding as other releases, but they are still releases.

"Love is the sea in which intellect drowns." ~Rumi.

Chapter 17 The Seven Seas

The Seven Seas is a saying used in ancient times to refer to the seven large bodies of water known. The term appears as early as 2300 BC in Hymn 8 of the Sumerian Enheduanna to the goddess Inanna. The Mesopotamians kept records of the observed seven moving objects in the heavens – the seven Classical Planets/Seven Heavens – and they made this connection to their seven seas.

The Arabian Seven Seas were often consisted of: the Black Sea, the Caspian Sea, the Arabian Sea, the Indian Ocean, the Red Sea, the Mediterranean Sea and the Adriatic Sea. However, now days we consider the seven seas to consist of: the Pacific Ocean, the Atlantic Ocean, the Indian Ocean, the Arctic Ocean, the Mediterranean Sea, the Caribbean Sea, and the Gulf of Mexico.

Each ocean, each of body of water has its own unique properties. Most, but not all of the "seas" consist of salt water. While Salt Water is ultimately undrinkable, it does have healing properties. Tears, like all salt water, can heal, but it too much can be deadly like in The Dead Sea. Visit to the Dead Sea can be healing and helpful, there is even a spa nearby. The problem is, things that are in the Dead Sea too long become consumed and killed. It is the same with the salt of our tears, tears are healthy, but dwell too long in them and they will consume you, you too will be a Dead Sea

The Black Sea is black because it has a fresh water lid. Fresh water pours in from a river, but cannot sink to the bottom. The denser salt water is kept at the bottom, and light cannot penetrate this dark, dense water, and so everything at the bottom dies and decays. This creates the black color.

What can we learn from this emotionally? If you repress your emotions then you are killing yourself off emotionally. New emotions will build on top of the old strong emotions and create a sort of lid. This emotional lid will keep you from even being able to deal with the old emotions. You will only be able to see the new problems and emotions without ever getting to the root of them. This causes you to become a very dark person emotionally, and it will show physically. Your Black Sea will show up in how you dress and the kind of music you listen to---your general life style and attitude.

The Caspian Sea is often considered the world's largest lake, though it contains salt water like an ocean. Because of its location and geologic history, it is rich with natural resources such as coal, gas and oil. However, the Caspian Sea has been damaged and polluted by the excess amounts of industry it has supported over the years.

Emotionally, we see the Caspian Sea as a symbol of using up all of our inner resources and polluting ourselves with toxic relationships. We begin life with so much love and energy to give to ourselves and to those around us, but when we don't respect our limits and boundaries, it can cause breakdowns. Eventually we won't be able to support ourselves, let alone others.

The Mederterian Sea is what is known as an "inland" sea. It is not completely isolated from the Atlantic, as it connects through the Straits of Gibraltar, but it is often considered its own body of water. The shores of the Mederterian are the site of many ancient cities. The ancients knew that water was life and that port cities were great places trade and for military strategy.

The ancients knew, intuitively, that water was to physical life as oceans were to emotional life. The ancient began their emotional journeys and their exploration of the world of emotions in the Mederterian. A journey across the sea became a symbol for struggle, adventure and growth. It is no coincidence that Odysseus spent so much time wandering across the ocean in The Odyssey.

Now, the ocean can be traveled in a three dimensional way. You can travel by latitude and longitude—horizontally and vertically—or you can travel from top to bottom. Emotions are like that as well. You can choose to move any direction, exploring any number of events, thoughts, or feelings that are out there. You can move through emotions in any area inside you. You can even move through emotions from past lives!

Since ancient times, people have always been curious what lay beneath the surface of our oceans and what lay beneath our emotions. It is only natural that we developed ways to explore these hidden depths with our body and minds over the centuries. First came the diving bell , which was one of the earliest types of equipment for underwater work and exploration. Its use was first described by Aristotle in the 4th century BC. It was improved upon in the 1600s. Finally, in the early 1900s we developed more sophisticated equipment to allow us to explore the ocean more freely. SCUBA stands for Self-Contained Breathing Apparatus. A tank full of oxygen strapped to the diver's back, along with a special mouth piece, allow divers to spend extended periods of times swimming underwater.

Similarly, with the advent of Psychology and exposure to various schools of thought around the world, we have many more sophisticated tools at our disposal for exploring our emotions. It is up to us to take advantage of the wealth of material we have access to and learn from it. Just as we can look at pictures and films of other people's deep sea dives, we can look at other people's inner explorations. Although self-help books can be helpful, I found it was really the biographies, autobiographies and diaries that I most benefited from in my search. Of course, nothing beats launching your own exploration, but in this age of information, we can no longer claim ignorance in not knowing where to begin. There are many, many, many examples out there to use.

Divers, however, can suffer from Rapture the Deep this when they descend into the sea too fast. This causes the nitrogen to build up in the blood stream and then the diver will feel like they are drunk essentially. There is euphoria, hallucinations, and loss of muscle control and shaking.

Emotionally people can experience this as well. If you allow yourself to dive into your emotions too quick then it can backfire. You will be overwhelmed with joy perhaps and completely in love, but then you lose control and start to see things that aren't there. Rapture the deep can be compared to letting your passion consume you, which can be very dangerous. If you descend into the ocean, into emotion, slowly, you still get to where you are going; it just may take a little longer. Patience is the key here.

"Someday, after mastering the winds, the waves, the tides and gravity, we shall harness for God the energies of love, and then, for a second time in the history of the world, man will have discovered fire." ~Pierre Teilhard de Chardin

Chapter 17 Fire

Water and Fire seem to be opposites and yet they coexist. Deep within the ocean there weak spots in the crust that give way to magma beneath. Eruptions can and do happen underwater, but not with as much force as we see on land. Sometimes we hear thunderous claps and watch as lava is projected high into the sky in a fiery fountain when a volcano erupts on land. But what happens when the water is there to temper it?

Fire and Water shape each other and know the power of give and take. The fire is raw power creation that motivate both our thoughts and our feelings. When magma is pushed through the ocean floor, it is met with great resistance. The cool temperatures quickly harden the outer shell. Then the inside begins to cool. When the flow breaks off and new one begins, we are left with what looks like pillows of rock along the ocean floor.

Lava is interesting because it is liquid or molten rock. It begins its life extremely hot and fluid, but when exposed to water and air, it quickly becomes hardened. It can flow like a thick river of water and it can the solid ground or foundation upon which we build things. It is both the destroyer and the creator.

There are many types of lava that have different consistencies and are made up of different minerals. Most are given Hawaiian names. Just as lava is varied, so is our creative mediums. We can be creative with writing, painting, drawing, sculpting, singing, dancing and so many other things. We can even be creative within the narrow boundaries of work, school and home. Anytime you solve a problem or craft something new out of whatever you have at your disposal, you are being creative.

Emotionally, the fire is creativity because very powerful. We do not always understand it or see it working in our lives in its rawest forms because emotions tend to cool and filter these creative urges, giving shape to them eventually.

Passion, Desire and Sexuality are all tied to creativity. It is the primal urge let life flow and continue through us. Rather we leave behind a bit of ourselves in our writing or rather we leave behind a part of ourselves in our children, we are giving into that creative urge to add to our existence and the existence of others.

The pillow formations on the ocean floor represent the places in which we have been changed by that creation. The more we change the world, the more we are changed by it. Rather it is in our subconscious, in dreams, or on the page, the force of creativity is always present.

"Thought is the wind and knowledge the sail."

~ David Hare

Chapter 18 The Wind

Wind is the perceptible natural movement of the air, especially in the form of a current of air blowing from a particular direction. Wind is caused by the differences in air pressure. Air under high pressure moves toward areas of low pressure. The greater the difference in pressure, the faster the air flows. This not unlike the movement of heat seeking an equilibrium.

Usually the creation of wind begins with the sun's radiation, which is absorbed differently on the earth's surface by different types of landscapes. Cloud cover, mountains, valleys, lakes, rivers, oceans, vegetation and desert lands all absorb radiation differently.

Generally wind is categorized by direction and speed. We can experience anything from a gentle breeze to strong winds when we step outside. Gale force winds can cause a great deal of damage, just as obsessively strong thoughts can do a great deal of damage our emotions. Pain, anger, rage and fear can cause internal tornados, hurricanes and typhoons. Our thoughts often create these emotional storms.

Although stirring up emotions into a fury and let loose can cause a storm, it can also be a healthy build up and release of tension. The wind blows constantly across the sea, as thoughts always drift across our mind. They are always pushing and pulling us one way or the other. These thoughts are what create the waves of emotion inside of us.

There wind is always moving along the shore because water and air cool at different rates. During the day, when the sun is up, the land heats up very quickly and the air above it warms up a lot more than the air over the water. The warm air over the land is less dense and begins to rise. Low pressure is created. Then the air pressure over the water is higher with cold dense air, which moves to occupy the space created over the land. The cool air that comes along is called a sea breeze.

At night, the reverse happens. The land quickly loses its heat whiles the water retains its warmth. This means the air over the water is warmer and the less dense and begins to rise. Low pressure is created over the water and so the cold and dense air over the land begins to move to the water surface to replace the warmer rising air. The cool breeze from the land is called a land breeze.

Emotionally we see things stir inside us at an unequal rate. Sometimes our thoughts are ahead of our emotions. We may understand something logically, but it takes time for our emotions to catch on. Other times we feel a subtle, but profound change in our emotions without understanding why. It may take time and reflection to see how and why there has been this unconscious shift.

Along with Sea Breezes and Land Breezes, there are the Polar Winds that circle the extremes of Earth and our emotions. They are the cold and slow winds that go round and round in circles around the top of the earth. Eventually, the air makes its way down into the

Prevailing Easterlies or the Prevailing Westerlies. Then the Trade Winds carry us toward the center of all things—the equator. They are thoughts that center us and calm us.

Doldrums are the very low pressure area along the equator where prevailing winds are calmest. This low pressure area is caused by the constant heating of the sun. When we are in an emotional doldrums, we are in a quiet place. That quiet, low pressure place can be a paradise or it can be hell. It just depends on the situation. The lack of wind—the lack of energy and thoughts—can be a good place to rest. Many times when someone is depressed they will describe it as being down in the doldrums. Being in this low place is natural part of our emotional life, but careful not to get stuck there. We need to get back to the Trade Winds eventually.

We also can't forget the Coriolis Effect. As the winds blow from the north and south towards the equator, their flow path is deflected by the earth's rotation. When moving objects are viewed in a reference frame, their path looks curved. The Coriolis Effect, is simply caused the earth's rotation. This effect makes wind systems in the southern side of the equator spin clockwise and wind systems in the northern side spin counter-clockwise.

What this means for us internally is that our physical body is always moving and changing and that it will have an effect on our thoughts, and in turn, our emotions. If we get sick it may bring us down or if we are healthy we may feel happy. By the same token, if we are depressed we may have physical ailments manifest because of it and if we are happy we may get healthier quicker. There is most definitely a mind-body connection.

But be mindful that thoughts alone cannot always change our physical body. Sometimes we need an outside source such as medicine to aid in our recovery.

"Nothing is softer or more flexible than water, yet nothing can resist it." ~Lao Tzu

Chapter 19 Surfing

The term *surfing* refers to the act of riding a wave, regardless of whether the wave is ridden with a board or without a board, and regardless of the stance used.

It was the Polynesians who originated the practice and the sport of riding the waves of the ocean. They were first observed doing so in the late 1700s and early 1800s. Surfing became a sport in the early 1900s, but hit its crest of popularity in the 1960s. Many surfers claim to have a spiritual connection with the ocean, describing surfing, the surfing experience, both in and out of the water, as a type of spiritual experience or a religion.

Surfing is the perfect metaphor for what we do with our emotions. So many times I have been told to control my emotions and somehow discipline them, but I have never been able to find a way to do so. If you have ever tried and failed to contain a particularly strong feeling, you know that trying to control emotions is like trying to control the ocean—impossible.

You may be able to contain the emotion or build levies to prevent them from overflowing, but you can't stop the water from flowing. The more water there is, the more difficult it is to even try to move it where you want it.

Surfers know you can't move the waves, but you can learn to anticipate where they are going and work with them. The same holds true for emotions. You can anticipate emotions and work with them as a surfer works with the waves.

The surfer learns how the ocean works and gets a feel for the mechanics of the waves. They gain an almost intuitive sense the best way to stay on top of things or how to get through them unscathed. They understand the Physics of the Ocean and its waves in a Zen-like state of awareness.

Height of the wave, the rate at which it is moving and weather conditions all factor into anticipating the ride. Once they paddle out into the ocean, they judge rather the waves are from deep in the ocean or if they are shallow shore waves and ride accordingly.

As a surfer of emotions you too can learn to identify what you are feeling and the affect it will have on you. You can observe the emotions tumbling inside you and how your thoughts change the speed and direction of those feelings. You can understand how it all comes together and you can anticipate what will happen next even if you can't control it.

Eventually you will not see your emotions as some mysterious, immovable force that you struggle with. Eventually you will see your emotions as something you can be connected to and in harmony with. Once you cultivate this understanding, you will have much better luck seeing everything from the tiniest detail of what triggers certain feelings to the overall big picture of your path.

"Human Love is not a substitute for Spiritual Love. It is an extension of it." ~Emmanuel

Chapter 20 The Seven Levels of Love

Love is love ultimately. It is pure divine energy. The problem is that our relationships often don't last long enough to experience love in its purest states. There is a debate on whether love at first sight is possible. Some psychologists and skeptics believe that love can only exist in a long-term mature relationship based on trust and respect. Some would even argue that love doesn't exist. Bitter and jaded, love's harshest critics claim that only lust exists. Physical urges make the world go round. Love is merely a romantic notion to the practical and the prejudice. We have poetry because it fulfills a need we have to believe in love. Some would say the idea of love is as empty as the idea of God.

I've heard it all and I choose to believe in both a divine source and collective unconscious. I even believe in love at first sight. Over the years though, I've refined my perceptions. Experience has not destroyed my belief in love; it has merely demanded some revision and amendments to my personal codex. Here is my way of explaining love's progression.

It is really all about widening and deepening our perceptions. When we meet someone, we recognize the soul. This is how we can love someone instantly. Love then exists in the *Atomic Stage*. It is a particle, a possibility. When two people actually connect, then love is in its *Electrical Stage*. When a couple makes love or has sex, then it is in its *Volcanic Stage*. It is fiery, passionate and powerful. Then slowly it evolves into a fertile *Garden Stage*. This stage is a place of growth and development. A relationship that lasts more than a few weeks or few months moves into this rich spot. When a couple survives the changes that they go through over the years, then they can consider themselves part of the *Earthly Stage*. It is time to settle down, get married and have kids during this time. This is mature love. When we open our hearts and learn to be completely vulnerable, we reach the *Oceanic Stage*. Oceanic love leads then to the *Cosmic Stage*. The Cosmic Stage is a spiritual love. This is a sense of timelessness and divinity.

All of your needs can be fulfilled and all of the stages can be reached, but it isn't common or easy to do so. Some relationships will only hit some of the stages. It is a rare relationship indeed that hits all of them. The romantic notion that we have only one chance at love seems to go hand in hand with the idea that we have only one life to lead. We lead many symbolic lives, and perhaps many actual lives. Why not have many actual loves? To say someone could not love someone they know briefly or perhaps even never met is to discount the Atomic and Cosmic Stages of love.

There is more to love than just reproduction, just as there is more to emotions than chemical reactions. I ask what good are chemical reactions without the intellect to comprehend them or the physical body to enjoy them. And without our faith how could we ever hope to reach the spiritual level of love? I'm not sure we could reach those levels without the element of faith, nor would I want to live without faith. I wouldn't like to live in a place without love or limit my definitions of love. If we need spiritual connections and spiritual love, why can't it already exist for us?

Appendix A:

The Metaphor of the Desert in *The English Patient*

The desert is vital to the narrative in Michael Ondaatje's *The English Patient*. The desert is parallel to the characters and even embodies them symbolically—more specifically it embodies the characters' romances and relationships. The desert metaphor can be broken down into three parts. There are the rocks that represent the stable soul, which is rooted firmly in place. Then you have the winds that are parallel to the path of life, which could be described as the life force. Finally, there are the shifting sands, which are the events of our lives. These sands are care carried by the life force, which carves and shapes the landscape around them.

The English Patient, Count László de Almásy, embodies the desert in all of its parts. The desert was once a great sea, full of life. Almásy also came to the desert full of life—a virtual sea of possibility. Then the desert began to change him and wipe out his previous identity ever so slowly. He travels to the desert to map it, but he is actually mapping his own soul. He feels at home in the desert and thus with himself. Katherine is one of the strong winds that carved away at him, shaping him into a new man. Their love affair changed their lives—their very identity—forever. The winds of passion quickly changed to the winds of death, bring up the theme of Eros and Thanatos—the intertwining of love and death. Almásy finds that love and death exists in his inner landscape. He realizes this when he tells his lover Katherine about *Felhomaly*. "The dusk of graves. With the connotation of intimacy there between the dead and the living." (170) As he lay dying in the Italian Villa, the winds sweep him from his life to his afterlife, continuing the endless cycle. He becomes a harbinger or reminder of this cycle for Caravaggio, Kip and Hana.

Hana is one of the strong rocks that scatter the landscape, silent and still. Her young life is quickly shaped by the violent winds of war and death. The wind has torn away her protection, so she is quite vulnerable. There is a sense of pain, loss and grieving that emanates from her. Hana is feeling the isolation and vastness of the desert in her own soul. It is the presence of this English Patient, Caravaggio and Kip that allows her to go through a kind of rebirth. The winds have torn her down, but now they are reshaping her into a new woman. Her relationship with Kip is like an oasis in her desert. For a time the heat of passion takes away her thirst and restores her. Then the water of Kip no longer sustains her. She finds herself searching more for what Kip represents to her than Kip himself.

Kip is like the sand itself, drifting and shifting without ever really changing. He is carried by the life force from one place to another and has no roots or attachments. In Eastern Philosophy this is the ideal state for a person to obtain. Kip has found himself in a new situation in the Italian Villa, which he observes and accesses from a distance. This distance gives him a sense of harmony as described in the novel, "Everything is gathered by him as a part of an altering harmony." (219) Kip is drawn to Hana to shape her in a different way—to soften her sharp edges. The wind that moves him is not violent, but quiet in reflective. It is the *Imbat Wind*.

Caravaggio is most like one of the many rocks in the desert, but he has been shaped by a very bitter wind known as the *Samiel Wind*. This man has always been a jagged and broken rock, but the winds of war have nearly made him crumble. When he encounters Hana, a different wind begins to shape him—the *Datto Wind*. The winds that had once been harsh, have now softened and are gentle. The need to care for and protect Hana has softened his own rough edges. Caravaggio lets go of himself a bit, the broken pieces of him being picked up by the wind and carried away. Those bits of him are now apart of the winds that affects those around him. He ties them together physically and metaphorically. The winds of passion, love and death are all flowing through him and around him. This affects his relationship not only to others, but with himself as well.

Almásy, like the desert itself, is the main character in the novel The English Patient. Hana and Caravaggio are two rocks standing in that vast desert—alone and yet connected. Finally, Kip is the ever-shifting sand that follows the life-force effortlessly. All of these poetic symbols create a landscape of the human soul that demonstrates the subtle changes within. Mapping the journey of spiritual growth is one that requires this kind of poetic imagery to get its point across, which Michael Ondaatje does beautifully.

Appendix B:

Overview

1. Emotion is Energy
2. Love is Light
3. Love is Electricity
4. Fear is Antimatter and Love is Matter
5. Fire is Creativity
6. Heat is Desire
7. Earth is Our Physical Body
8. Wind is our Thoughts
9. Ocean is our Emotions
10. Islands in the Sea are our Projections or Mirrors.

Consciousness is Knowledge and Awareness

Joy, Sadness, Anger and Disgust are Elemental Feelings

Beware of Displaced Anger that Causes Chaos and Entropy

We all need an Anchor or Constant in our lives.

The World is a Mirror from which we see ourselves most clearly.

Relationships are Uncertain and the Outcomes cannot be predicted.

If Only or Counterfactuals Can Help Us See What Was, Is, Will Be.

You can't Control Your Feelings, Only Understand Them

Everything is connected. We are all connected.

Don't Cut Yourself Off From Your Feelings.

Issues can keep us Stuck or Going in Circles.

Embrace the Darkness. It can transform you for the Better.

The Only Way Out is Through.

Appendix C:

List of Emotions

Aristotle was a Greek Philosopher that lived 384–322 BC. He was the one who first laid out a list of emotions in his work on Rhetoric. He says we feel: **Anger, Fear, Shame, Kindness, Pity, Indignation, Envy, Jealousy**, and **Love**.

Robert Plutchik (1927-2006) was professor emeritus at the Albert Einstein College of Medicine and adjunct professor at the University of South Florida. He received his Ph.D. from Columbia University and he was also a psychologist. Robert Plutchik's theory says that the eight basic emotions are: **Fear, Anger, Sadness, Joy, Disgust, Trust, Surprise** and **Anticipation.** He developed a wheel that shows the relationships between emotions. He paired them into bipolar pairs: He suggested eight primary bipolar emotions: joy versus sadness; anger versus fear; trust versus disgust; and surprise versus anticipation.

Perhaps my favorite list is the *23 Obscure Words for Emotions You Never Realized Anyone Felt* by John Koenig.

Adronitis: Frustration of how long it takes to get to know someone.

Altshmerz: Weariness with the same old issues you've always had and with the same anxieties you've been gnawing on for years.

Clinomania: An excessive desire to stay in bed.

Chrysalism: The amniotic tranquility of being indoors during a storm.

96

Ellipsism: Sadness that you'll never be able to know how history will turn out.

Enoument: Bitter sweetness of having arrived in the future, seeing how things turn out, but not being able to tell your past self.

Exulansis: The tendency to give up trying to talk about an experience because people are unable to relate to it.

Gerful: Wild and Wayward.

Jouska: A hypothetical conversation that you compulsively play out in your head over and over.

Keubuko: The state of exhaustion inspired by acts of senseless violence.

Kenopsia: The eerie forlorn atmosphere of a place that is usually busy with people, but is now abandoned and quiet.

Lachesism: Desire to be struck by disaster and survive.

Liberosis: Desire to care less about things.

Mauerbauertraurigkeit: Inexplicable urge to push people away—even close friends that you really like.

Monochopsis: A subtle, but persistent feeling of being out of place.

Nodus Tollons: The realization that the plot of your life doesn't make sense to you anymore.

Occhiolism: The awareness of the smallness of your perspective.

Onism: The frustration of being stuck in just one body that inhabits one place at a time.

Opia: The ambiguous intensity of looking someone in the eye, which can feel simultaneously feel invasive and vulnerable.

Rubatosis: The unsettling awareness of your own heartbeat.

Saorsa: Freedom or liberty.

Sonder: The realization that each passer-by has his or her own life that you are not privy to and that is as complex and vivid as your own.

Vellichor: The strange wistfulness of used bookshelves.

Some of my favorite words to describe feelings that I discovered along the way came from other languages as well.

Mono No Aware: Is Japanese for Tinge of Sadness that permeates life even if good times.

Sehnsucht: Is German for Hunger or a Longing for that which cannot be named or obtained.

BIBLIOGRAPHY

Bly, Robert, *The Maiden King: The Reunion of The Masculine and the Feminine*. Henry Holt and Co, 1998.

Capra, Fritjof, *The Tao of Physics: An Exploration of the Parallels Between Modern Physics and Eastern Mysticism*. Shambala, 2010.

Chodron, Pema, *The Places That Scare You: A Guide To Fearlessness in Difficult Times*. Shambala, 2002.

Chodron, Pema, *When Things Fall Apart: Heart Advice for Difficult Times*. Shambala, 2000

Chodron, Pema, *The Wisdom of No Escape and the Path of Loving Kindness*. Shambala, 2001.

Edinger, Edward, *The Ego and Archetype*: Shambala, 1992.

Gawain, Shakti. *Living In The Light*. Nataraja 1993.

Greene, Brian. *The Elegant Universe: Superstrings, Hidden Dimensions and the Quest For The Ultimate Theory*. W.W. Norton, 2010.

Griscom, Chris, *Ecstasy is a New Frequency: Teachings of The Light Institute, Fireside, 1988*.

Gyatso, Bstan-'dzin-rgya-mtsho (His Holiness The Dalai Lama) And Carter, Howard. *The Art of Happiness. A Handbook for Living*. New York: Riverhead, 1998.

Hamer, Dean. *The God Gene: How Faith Is Hardwired Into Our Genes*. Doubleday, 2004.

Hawking, Stephen. *A Brief History of Time*. Bantam, 1998.

Hawking, Stephen. *Grand Design*. Bantam, 2012.

Irvine, William B, *On Desire*: *Why We Want What We Want.* Oxford Press, 2007.

Jung, Carl, *Archetypes of the Unconscious: Collected Works of Jung, Volume 9 Part 1.* Princeton University Press, 1981.

Johnson, Steve, *Mind Wide Open: Your Brain and the Neuroscience of Everyday Life.* Scribner, 2004.

Kaku, Michio, *Physics of the Future: Science in the Year 2100.* Anchor 2012.

Kaku, Michio. *Physics of the Impossible.* Anchor Books, 2008.

Kelly, Mathew. *The Seven Levels of Intimacy. Fireside, 2005.*

Kornfield, Jack. *A Path with Heart: A Guide Through the Perils and Promises of Spiritual Life.* Bantam, 1993.

Kramer, Peter. *Against Depression.* Viking, 2005.

Lederman, Leon. *The God Particle: If the Universe is the Answer, What is the Question?* Mariner Reprint, 2006.

Myss, Carolyn. *The Anatomy of the Spirit: The Seven Stages of Power and Healing.* Harmony, 1997.

Moore, Thomas, *Dark Night of the Soul: A Guide For Finding Your Way Through Life's Ordeals.* Gotham, 2005.

Norretranders, Tor, *The User Illusion: Cutting Consciousness Down To Size.* Penguin, 1999.

Ondaatje, Michael. *The English Patient.* Vintage, 1993.

Roese, Neal, *If Only: How To Turn Regret into Opportunity,* Harmony, 2011.

Stitskin, Nahum. *The Looking Glass God: Shinto, Yin and Yang and Cosmology for Today.* Autumn Press, 1972.

Starhawk, *Dreaming The Dark.* Beacon Press, 1982.

Starhawk, *Truth or Dare: Encounters with Power, Authority and Mystery. HarperOne, 1989.*

Starhawk, *The Twelve Wild Swans*: *A Journey To the Realm of Magic, Healing and Action.* Harper One. 2001.

Tyson, Neil deGrasse. *Origins: Fourteen Billion Years of Evolution.* W.W. Norton, 2014.

Tyson, Neil deGrasse. *Space Chronicles: Facing The Ultimate Frontier.* W.W. Norton, 2014.

Walker, Evan Harris, *The Physics of Consciousness*: *The Quantum Mind and the Meaning of Life.* Basic Books, 2000.

Woodman, Marion and Dickson, Elinor, *Dancing in the Flames: The Dark Goddess in The Transformation of Consciousness. Shambala, 1997.*

Woodman, Marion*, The Pregnant Virgin: A Psychological Process of Transformation* (Studies in Jungian Psychology). Inner City Books, 1991

Zukav, Gary, *The Dancing Wu Li* Masters: *An Overview of the New Physics.* Bantam Books, 1980.

Made in the USA
Middletown, DE
16 January 2018